COMMUNITIES OF LIFE

Deserts

JANE HURWITZ

PERFECTION LEARNING®

Editorial Director: Susan C. Thies
Editor: Mary L. Bush
Design Director: Randy Messer
Book Design: Brianne Osborn, Emily J. Greazel
Cover Design: Michael A. Aspengren

A special thanks to the following for their scientific review of the book:
Paul Pistek, Instructor of Biological Sciences, North Iowa Area Community College
Jeffrey Bush, Field Engineer, Vessco, Inc.

For Freda, who is the "desert" sunshine of my life

For information, contact
Perfection Learning® Corporation
1000 North Second Avenue, P.O. Box 500
Logan, Iowa 51546-0500.
Phone: 1-800-831-4190
Fax: 1-800-543-2745
perfectionlearning.com

2 3 4 5 6 PP 08 07 06 05 04

Paperback ISBN 0-7891-6015-3
Reinforced Library Binding ISBN 0-7569-4462-7

Contents

Introduction 4

Chapter 1 The Desert 8

Chapter 2 Desert Locations 12

Chapter 3 Deserts of the World 18

Chapter 4 Life in the Desert 26

Chapter 5 News from the Desert 32

Internet Connections and Related Reading for Deserts 36

Glossary 38

Index 40

Introduction

If someone asked you to describe the area where you live, what would you say? Do you live in a desert region where it's hot and dry? a forest area with lots of evergreen trees? near a hot, wet tropical rain forest? How would you describe the temperature, sunlight, and rainfall in your hometown? What plants and animals live there?

Biomes

You are describing a biome. A biome is an **environment** with unique features. For example, an ocean biome has salt water. A **tundra** biome is cold and dry, and often the ground is frozen year-round.

There are many types of biomes, including desert, mountain, tundra, forest, grassland, ocean (saltwater), freshwater, and rain forest. Ecologists have noticed that the same biomes can appear in very different places. Deserts, for example, are found in both hot and cold locations. But even though they are in different parts of the world, all deserts share some characteristics.

Biome Career

Ecologists are scientists who study the relationship between the Earth and the living things on the planet.

Small plants and animals live on coral reefs in the ocean.

Waterfalls flowing through the layers of the rain forest provide moisture for the many green plants growing there.

Each biome has its own special plant life. Think about the different plants found in a desert, a rain forest, and a grassland. Cactuses grow in the desert. Palm trees grow in the rain forest. A variety of grasses cover the grassland.

Biomes are also identified by how plants and animals must **adapt** in order to live there. To live in an ocean biome, plants and animals must be able to live in salt water. In a desert, the wildlife must be able to survive long periods without water. Each biome has its own unique environment to which the plants and animals must adapt.

Ecosystems

Ecologists have also determined that certain groups of plants and animals tend to live together. These groups of living creatures interact with the nonliving parts of the environment, such as rocks or sand. Groups of living creatures that interact with one another and their surroundings are called *ecosystems*.

Each biome is made up of many ecosystems. In an ocean, there are different ecosystems living in **coral reefs**, cold Arctic waters, and deep underwater **trenches**. Each layer of a tropical rain forest has its own ecosystems.

Working together, the ecosystems form **communities** of life within each of the biomes.

Chapter 1

The Desert

What do you think of when you hear the word *desert*? Most people think of a hot, sandy place where nothing grows. Perhaps you think the desert is a place where it never rains. Many deserts do fit these descriptions, but there are several other kinds of deserts too.

A desert is defined as an area of land that is very dry. Less than ten inches of **precipitation** falls on the ground each year. Notice that the definition doesn't mention temperature or type of land. This means that deserts can be cold as well as hot. It also means that deserts do not have to be covered in sand. In fact, some deserts are rocky.

A few deserts are even covered in snow and ice. Antarctica is a desert because it only receives a few inches of precipitation a year. Because of the cold temperatures, the moisture falls as snow. The total amount of precipitation equals less than ten inches of water per year.

Flowers bloom on this desert cactus.

The Desert Biome

Desert biomes can be found all over the world. North America has four deserts—the Great Basin, Mojave, Sonoran, and Chihuahuan. The Patagonia and Atacama Deserts are found in South America. Asia is home to the Thar, Gobi, Arabian, Takla Makan, and Turkestan Deserts. The Sahara and Kalahari Deserts are located in Africa. The small island **continent** of Australia has four major deserts—the Great Victoria, the Great Sandy, the Simpson, and the Gibson. The whole continent of Antarctica is a cold desert. Although these deserts are spread across the globe, they all share the same basic characteristics of a desert biome.

Plants and animals in the desert biome must adapt to the environment. They must be able to live with very little water. Most desert animals cannot depend on plant life as a steady diet of food. Those that do rely on plants must eat the special kinds of plants found in the desert.

Ecosystems in the Desert

Desert biomes are large areas of land where plants and animals have adapted to low rainfall. But because temperatures and land

features can vary, deserts around the world can be very different from one another. Antarctica is a cold desert with snow and ice. The Arabian Desert in Asia is a hot desert covered almost entirely with sand. The Chihuahuan Desert in the United States is covered with stony areas, sandy soil, and many mountains and **mesas**.

The plants and animals that make up each desert's ecosystems are as different as the deserts themselves. Antarctica is home to penguins and only a few shrubs and grasses. Camels and oleander are familiar sights in the Arabian Desert. Coyotes, kangaroo rats, and roadrunners travel across the Chihuahuan land, where cactuses and Mexican gold poppies grow.

The differences in the deserts' ecosystems make these communities unique areas worth exploring!

Rats As Big As Kangaroos?

Kangaroo rats are small animals with long tails that hop like kangaroos. These rats use their strong hind legs to hop, dig, and protect themselves. They are active at night and spend hot desert days in their **burrows**. Kangaroo rats eat seeds, which contain the little water they need to survive.

Plants of the Desert

Oleander is a blooming plant that can live in a variety of soils and thrives in heat. This poisonous plant can have white, pink, red, or yellow flowers.

The Mexican gold poppy is a small wildflower with orange or gold cup-shaped flowers.

Pink oleander

Chapter 2

Desert Locations

T he Earth is divided into seven continents. Deserts are found on six of these seven continents. Europe is the only continent with no deserts. About one-fifth of the land on Earth is desert.

Where on Earth Are We?

The globe is divided with invisible lines to help locate places. One set of lines runs up and down the Earth. They are called *lines of longitude*. The other set of lines runs around the Earth like imaginary belts. These are called *lines of latitude*.

The most famous line of latitude is the equator. The equator runs around the middle of the Earth. It is halfway between the North Pole and the South Pole.

North Pole

Equator

South Pole

Where Are the Deserts?

Climate is the weather found in an ecosystem. In a desert ecosystem, the climate is dry. The desert climate may include some rain or snow, but not much. When rain or snow does fall in a desert area, other types of weather cause the land to remain dry. Wind or heat can cause any precipitation to **evaporate** quickly.

Because the equator receives a lot of sunlight, the land there has hot weather year-round. The climate surrounding the equator is called *tropical*. Tropical climates are warm and moist for most of the year.

The climate changes as you move north or south of the equator. The differences between the seasons become more noticeable. Temperatures and precipitation vary at different times of the year.

The northern and southern boundaries of the tropical region are marked by two lines of latitude. The northern boundary is called the Tropic of Cancer. The southern boundary is called the Tropic of Capricorn. These two latitude rings mark the change from the hotter climates to the milder, or **temperate**, climates. At the Tropics, the climate is subtropical. This means it isn't as hot and wet as it is at the equator, but it is still warmer than

temperate climates. It is in these subtropical areas that deserts are most likely to form.

Subtropical Deserts

Most of the region around the equator is covered by oceans. Air above the equator is warmed by the Sun. As the Sun warms the air, it also evaporates water from the oceans. The warm air holds the moisture. This creates the equator's warm, wet climate.

As air moves away from the hot equator, it cools. Cool air doesn't hold as much moisture as warm air, so the moisture falls as rain. That's why tropical rain forests receive a lot of rain.

As the cooler air moves even farther away from the equator, it is drawn down and becomes wind. This wind is usually strongest over the Tropics of Cancer and Capricorn. Little moisture arrives with these winds, resulting in desert lands.

Three of the world's largest desert areas are located at the tropics. They are the four Australian deserts, the Arabian Desert, and the Sahara Desert. Several other deserts lie near these areas as well.

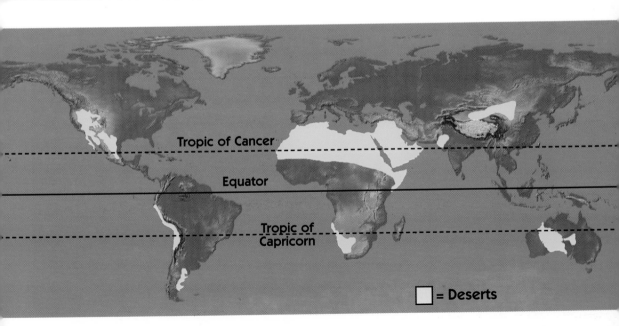

Tropic of Cancer

Equator

Tropic of Capricorn

☐ = Deserts

Rain Shadows

Not all deserts form just because they are near the Tropics of Cancer or Capricorn. Deserts may form for other reasons. The "rain shadow effect" explains one of the ways that some deserts form.

When wind blows into a mountain range, the mountains act as a **barrier**. The wind must rise to move over the mountains. As wind rises, it becomes colder. Since cold air cannot hold as much moisture as warm air, any water trapped in the air is squeezed out. This moisture falls on the mountains as rain or snow.

By the time the air has passed over the mountains, all of the moisture has been released. The air is very dry. The land on the far side of the mountains doesn't receive any rain or snow. A desert environment then forms in the rainless shadow of the mountains.

Unlike subtropical deserts, rain shadow deserts may form at any latitude. Where these deserts form depends entirely on wind patterns and the location of mountains.

All four deserts in the United States—the Mojave, Great Basin, Sonoran, and Chihuahuan—are affected by the rain shadow

Mojave Desert

effect. These deserts are trapped by the Cascade Mountains or Sierra Nevada to the west and the Rocky Mountains to the east. Parts of the Australian deserts were also created by the rain shadow effect.

Deserts Near Water

Although deserts are dry, some actually develop next to water. The Atacama Desert in Chile is next to the Pacific Ocean. From the Namib Desert in southern Africa, you can watch the waves in the Atlantic Ocean.

The Driest Place on Earth

The Atacama Desert is the driest desert on Earth. Brief rainfall may occur only once every 5–20 years.

When cold ocean **currents** flow near land, **coastal** deserts may form. Air over the ocean is cooled by the currents. As the cool ocean air flows toward the warmer air over the land, fog forms. Fog is actually a cloud that is floating very close to the ground. Like clouds, fog holds water. Even though the fog travels over the land, very little of the water is released. When the land doesn't get enough moisture over a long period of time, it becomes a desert.

Deserts Far from Water

Other deserts form because they are too far from a large source of water, such as an ocean. Air blowing over the ocean picks up water. This water is carried over the land in clouds. As the clouds pass over the land, water is dropped as rain or snow. By the time the clouds arrive at the center of a large continent, they have shed most or all of their water. Very little or no precipitation falls, creating a desert. The Gobi Desert in central Asia is one of these deserts located far from water.

Named for Stones

The Gobi Desert is covered with sandy soil and areas of small stones. These stones are called *gobi*.

Chapter 3

Deserts of the World

Deserts are found around the world. Besides location, they are often grouped by temperature. However, deserts with the same temperature patterns are not always located in the same part of the world.

Hot Deserts

You won't need a coat if you visit one of the hot deserts. These deserts are warm most of the year. In the summer, they can become unbearably hot. Some hot deserts are the Sahara in Africa, the Thar in Pakistan and India, and the Mojave in North America.

The Sahara Desert

The Sahara is the largest desert in the world. It covers about 3.5 million square miles. The entire Sahara would almost fill the same amount of land as the United States!

The Sahara is a subtropical desert located in northern Africa. It is surrounded by water on three of its borders—the Atlantic Ocean to the west, the Mediterranean Sea to the north, and the Red Sea to the east. To the south, the Sahara is bordered by land. There is a bit more moisture near this southern border.

Sandy Sahara?

Sand covers only about 12 percent of the Sahara Desert. Mountains, rocky **plateaus**, and gravelly **plains** make up the rest.

Temperatures in the Sahara average above 90°F in the summer. Some parts of the desert reach temperatures of 110°F or higher. The average yearly rainfall is less than eight inches with some areas receiving less than one inch. The temperature and lack of moisture make the Sahara a very hot, dry desert!

One animal that is famous for living in the extreme heat of the Sahara is the camel. In order to beat the heat, a camel's body temperature changes. When the air temperature rises, the camel's temperature rises to about 104°F. The increase in body temperature means the camel doesn't have to sweat or pant as much to stay cool. This saves water in the camel's body. At night, when the air temperature drops, the camel's temperature decreases to about 95°F.

For many hundreds of years, the only way to cross many deserts such as the Sahara was on camels. Groups of camels used for transportation were called *caravans*. The caravans would stop at a resting spot called an *oasis*. An oasis is a place in the desert where underground water rises to the earth's surface. This creates soil where trees and other plants can grow. It also creates a place for people to live. The oases were filling stations for the camel caravans on their journeys across the desert. Even though camel caravans have been replaced by trucks and airplanes today, people still live at the oases as they have for thousands of years.

The Thar

Camel caravans are still used in the Thar Desert. Located in parts of Pakistan and India, the Thar Desert is the world's seventh largest desert. It is almost the same size as the states of Louisiana and North Carolina combined.

The Thar receives less than ten inches of rain a year. The average summer temperature is about 80°F with many days reaching well above this temperature.

The Thar is a sandy desert. In fact, *Thar* means "sandy desert." Sand is often blown into large hills by the wind. These hills are called *dunes*. The wind speed and direction determine the size and shape of sand dunes. Not many large trees or plants can grow on sand dunes, so in the Thar Desert, most plants are small and grasslike.

The Mojave

Sand is not as common in the deserts of North America. Only about two percent of the North American deserts are covered in sand. Even though many plants cannot live on the shifting sand dunes, some creatures can. If you walk among the sand dunes of the Mojave Desert, be careful where you step! More than ten different types of scorpions live in the Mojave.

Besides sand, the Mojave landscape includes sandy soil, rocky areas, and gravel. Death Valley is located in the Mojave. Death Valley is a deep **trough** surrounded by steep slopes. The area is dry and **barren**, but beautiful to see.

In the summer, the daytime temperatures in the Mojave often rise over 100°F. Winter temperatures in the Mojave are mild. An average temperature of 55°F is normal.

It doesn't rain much in the Mojave—only about six inches a year. Even with so little rain, many plants manage to grow there. The creosote bush, brittle

Scorpions paralyze insects and small rodents with stingers on the tips of their tails.

bush, and desert holly are all common in the Mojave Desert. The Joshua tree grows in the Mojave. This tree has bell-shaped flowers and can reach up to 50 feet tall. The Joshua tree cannot be found anywhere else on Earth.

The dunes of the Mojave are also home to a small rattlesnake called the *sidewinder*. The sideways motion of the sidewinder is an **adaptation** to the hot sands. As it glides across the sand, only a small part of the sidewinder's body comes in contact with the burning sand at any one time.

Darkling beetle

Hot and Cold Deserts

Other deserts have both hot and cold seasons. Each season may have extreme temperatures. Often the hot season is very hot and the cold season is very cold. The Gobi Desert in Mongolia and the Namib Desert in Africa experience two different seasons.

The Namib

The Namib Desert in southern Africa is a very dry coastal desert. Large sand dunes cover the edges of this desert. The coast along the edge of the Namib is often called the "skeleton coast." Long ago, many shipwrecks occurred on Namib's coast due to the fast ocean current, thick fog, and powerful winds from the Atlantic Ocean. Those that survived the journey often died from the harsh desert conditions.

Some parts of the Namib receive only two inches of rain a year. While nights can be very cold, days are warm to extremely hot. In some inner areas of the Namib, temperatures soar to over 100°F.

The Oldest Desert in the World

The Namib is over 80 million years old and believed to be the oldest desert in the world.

Many animals with interesting names live in the Namib Desert. The darkling beetle is a black beetle with hard front wings. Some of these beetles defend themselves by standing on their heads and releasing a chemical with a horrible smell.

The fringe-toed lizard has several adaptations for living in the desert. Its coloring blends in with the sand, and its jaw, nostrils, ears, and eyelids are all designed to prevent sand from getting in. The lizard's fringed toes help push it through the sand.

The Namib web-footed gecko is colored brown or gray to blend in with its desert surroundings. Its skinny legs and large webbed feet help it run across sand and dig burrows. The web-footed gecko stays in its burrow during the hot days and only comes out at night when the temperatures are cooler.

Similar Snakes

The dwarf adder and Peringuey's adder are two small poisonous snakes that live in the Namib. They move like the sidewinder rattlesnake of the Mojave Desert. Although these snakes live in different parts of the world, they have adapted to desert life in similar ways.

Sidewinder rattlesnake

The Gobi

The Gobi Desert is another desert with hot and cold seasons. Unlike the Namib, the surface of the Gobi is mostly covered with rocks and gravel. Over three-fourths of the Gobi Desert is covered with plants. Grasses, small shrubs, and thorny bushes are common in the Gobi.

The Gobi Desert is the fifth largest desert in the world. It is located in Mongolia. Summer temperatures can reach 104°F. Winter temperatures of -40°F have been recorded. The Gobi receives less than eight inches of precipitation in the summer and two to three inches in the winter. Much of the summer rainwater evaporates due to the high temperatures.

Crossing the Gobi

A famous trade route from long ago passes through the Gobi Desert. It is called the Silk Road. This trade route was taken by the great explorer Marco Polo on his trip from Europe to China. The Gobi Desert is so large that it took Marco Polo nearly 30 days to cross it.

Cold Deserts

A few deserts always have cold temperatures. The temperature in cold deserts does rise somewhat in the summer. However, the summer season is short, and the temperature change isn't great. The warmer period does provide a short growing season for a few plants. Two examples of cold deserts are Antarctica and parts of Greenland.

Antarctica

It is strange to think that land covered in snow could be a desert. Yet, if the snow stays frozen and the land remains dry, a desert forms. Antarctica is one of the driest places on Earth. Very little precipitation, in the form of snow, falls.

Because Antarctica is far away from the equator, the Sun is never fully overhead. Therefore, this continent is almost entirely covered by a permanent layer of ice. Only two percent of the continent is ice-free. These ice-free areas are windy, rocky lands.

The Antarctic Desert has no shrubs or trees. It wasn't until the 1970s that scientists discovered that algae and fungi were living in the rocks of Antarctica. These **organisms** are only visible with a microscope. They live in between tiny gaps in the rocks found in ice-free areas. The algae and fungi are sheltered from the bitter cold. Yet they remain close enough to the surface of the rock to soak up the weak sunlight.

Any wildlife that calls this desert home must find food from the surrounding ocean. Seals and penguins manage to spend part of their lives on the Antarctic ice. There are six species of penguins that are **native** to Antarctica. The Emperor penguin is the largest. There are also six species of native seals. The leopard seal and the southern elephant seal are two common native seals. While seals find most of their food in the ocean, they will occasionally eat a penguin.

Greenland

At the opposite end of the Earth from Antarctica lies Greenland, the largest island in the world. This island lies in the **Arctic Circle**, where temperatures can reach -70°F in the winter. Only about 15 percent of Greenland is ice-free. Parts of Greenland are a frozen desert. These areas receive about 10 inches of snow each year. Because of the freezing temperatures, however, most of this precipitation stays frozen as snow or ice.

Greenland has many animals that can survive the desert cold. Musk ox are large mammals that have a double layer of fur. The outer layer is made of stiff hair that keeps out ice and snow. Underneath is a thick layer of softer fur that keeps the musk ox warm.

The arctic fox has thick fur and a bushy tail that keeps its nose and feet warm when it sleeps.

The arctic fox is another animal of Greenland with fur that helps it survive in the snowy desert. In the winter, the arctic fox's fur is white. This allows the fox to blend in with the snow, so prey have difficulty seeing it. When the spring comes, the fox sheds its white coat for a layer of brown fur, again providing a perfect **camouflage** against sand and soil.

Chapter 4

Life in the Desert

Imagine that you're walking across a hot desert. The sun beats down on the dry land. The ground burns your feet. There is little water or shade. As you look around, you notice that the plants look different from those in your neighborhood. Very few creatures are moving.

Perhaps you're traveling through a cold desert. The frigid, dry air is hard to breathe. Despite layers of heavy clothing, you're still shivering. All around, you see snow and ice. No plants or animals are in sight.

Can you imagine living in one of these deserts? Could you survive? Amazingly, plants, animals, and even people *do* survive in the tough desert environments. Creatures of the desert have special characteristics, or adaptations, to help them stay alive in the harsh ecosystems.

Plant Adaptations

Some areas in desert ecosystems cannot support plant life. Blowing sand and rocks do not give plant roots anything to hold on to. Frozen ground doesn't allow many plants to grow. Other areas do not have enough water for even the toughest plants.

But some plants have adapted over time. They are able to overcome the tough desert conditions.

Rain doesn't come often to the desert. In order to survive between rains, desert plants often develop special root systems. They grow long, deep roots. The roots travel far into the earth to absorb water from deep underground.

This creosote bush has adapted to life in a sand dune.

These root systems are common on desert trees and shrubs. The creosote bush found in North American deserts is one such tough plant.

In addition to deep roots, desert plants also develop large, thin root systems close to the surface. When rain does fall, the mat of shallow roots is able to quickly soak up as much moisture as possible. The creosote bush has these shallow roots as well as deep ones. It takes in as much water as possible from both root systems.

The creosote bush has small, leathery leaves adapted to the desert dryness. Smaller leaves lose less moisture under dry conditions. Tough, leathery leaves are less likely to be eaten by animals looking for food and water.

Many other desert plants have leaf adaptations. Acacias found in the Gibson Desert in Australia have small, tough leaves. Juniper trees that grow on the edges of the Sahara Desert in Africa have needles that are tough and lose very little water to the dry air.

Plants in all ecosystems use photosynthesis to create energy. Photosynthesis is the process of using sunlight, carbon dioxide, and water to make sugars. These sugars are used by the plants as a source of energy.

Of course, the desert has plenty of sunlight. Unfortunately, when the Sun is out and photosynthesis takes place, water may escape from the plant. In the desert, where water is scarce, this can strain the plant to the point of death. But some desert plants have adapted. Certain plants can start photosynthesis at night or during the cooler part of the day. They finish the energy-making process in the morning when the sun rises. This adaptation allows the plant to produce energy with a lower risk of water loss.

Cactuses are among the desert plants that work at night. They store carbon dioxide during the cooler nighttime temperatures. The next morning when sunlight returns to provide energy, photosynthesis can take place.

Cactuses have other desert adaptations too. They have developed thick stems that can hold large amounts of water. The prickly spines on cactuses also provide protection from animals that would otherwise drink the stored water.

Animal Adaptations

Animals must also adapt to the extreme temperatures and lack of water. Many reptiles and mammals adapt to the heat of the desert by avoiding it. They sleep or rest in the shade or in burrows during the day. At night, these creatures come out in search of food. Animals that are active at night are called *nocturnal*.

In the deserts of the southwestern United States, night brings out many hungry animals. Bobcats come out of their shaded hiding places to hunt for **rodents**. Desert tarantulas move to the entrances of their underground burrows. The tarantulas wait at the edges of their burrows until a beetle, small snake, or mouse comes close enough to attack. In the desert night, animals hunt and are hunted.

Sleep is another adaptation to avoid the heat. When the desert temperature is too high, some animals go into a very deep sleep. This sleep is called *estivation*. It is similar to **hibernation**. When desert animals estivate, their bodies slow down. They breathe less often. Their hearts beat more slowly. They do not need to eat every day. Instead of food, their bodies survive by using stored body fat for energy.

The Mojave ground squirrel estivates in July or August, when the desert temperatures climb. The squirrel moves into its underground burrow and enters a deep sleep. When temperatures are more bearable, the squirrel leaves its burrow in search of food.

Some desert animals have the ability to reduce body heat. Jackrabbits have large ears that release heat when the animal is resting. Birds, like vultures and storks, escape daytime heat by flying high into cooler air. Many desert animals have paler coloring than their relatives that live in other biomes. Pale colors don't absorb as much heat.

Bobcat

Desert animals also need ways to survive when water is scarce. Some creatures, such as toads, can hold on to moisture by burrowing into moist soil during the day. Others can get enough water from the foods they eat. Plants like cactuses are a source of water for certain desert animals. Many insects can suck liquids from plants or eat leaves and fruit that hold moisture.

Mammals are the most affected by the lack of water as they aren't able to hold much water. These animals need freshwater at least every few days. Because of this, mammals are scarce in many desert areas.

Desert Pets

The gerbils that many people keep as pets are native to the desert. They are common in cold deserts like the Gobi and Turkestan. They are also found in hot deserts such as the Kalahari.

Human Adaptations

Only one-eighth of the world's people live in deserts. Some have settled in oasis towns. Others wander from place to place. These wanderers are called *nomads*. Nomads don't build houses. Instead they live in tents and other easy-to-move shelters.

Nomadic Birds

Like humans, desert animals can also be nomadic. In the Gibson Desert of Australia, flocks of parakeets fly from place to place. They settle temporarily when they find water or grass seed to eat. The number of nomadic birds in a flock may be more than 1000.

The nomadic life is suited to the desert. When the water and plants are used up in one area, nomads move on to another area. Some nomads raise livestock, such as goats and sheep, for food. These nomads move on when their animals have eaten all the grazing plants in an area. Other nomads hunt animals for food and gather plants that they can eat. They move from place to place in search of new animal and plant sources.

The Kalahari Desert in southern Africa is home to the San people. The San are nomads who have lived in the Kalahari for thousands of years. Many think that early San people were the first humans to live in this part of Africa.

The San people are made up of many tribes. Each tribe has a slightly different language. One thing that all San people have in common is a "clicking" sound when they speak. The clicks are actually exclamation points in their speech.

The San people are hunters and gatherers. More than 80 percent of the food that the San people eat is gathered by the women of the tribe. There are over 200 varieties of plants that the San people have learned are safe to eat. In addition to nuts, berries, and roots, the women trap small animals. The San also eat lizards, snakes, and insects. Women often spend three full days a week gathering food from the desert. The men of the tribe hunt large animals when they are available.

As the seasons change, the San people wander from place to place. They follow animal herds. Centuries of adapting to the desert ecosystem have taught them where they can gather food during the Kalahari's driest spells.

The Mongolians of the Gobi Desert and the Bedouins of the Arabian Desert are two other nomadic groups.

San women in the Kalahari Desert

Chapter 5

News from the Desert

All ecosystems and biomes are connected. A change in one ecosystem will often affect a neighboring ecosystem. For example, if the temperatures in the ocean biome changed, how would that affect coastal deserts?

The desert biome, with its harsh climates, may seem less important than other parts of the Earth. Fewer people live in the desert. It also has fewer animals and plants. But the desert holds many resources—perhaps some that have yet to be discovered. It is also home to unique desert plant and animal life. The desert is an important part of the world community—one that needs to be understood and protected.

Desertification

Desertification is a special problem that is a danger to deserts. It happens when normal changes in the size of a desert speed up. Desertification is often a result of farming or overgrazing of animals.

Every day, the world's population grows. As more and more people need homes and food, there is pressure to use lands on the edge of the deserts. These are fragile areas. The soil is thin. There is little water. Plant roots hold the soil in place. When animals are allowed to eat too many of the plants, the soil blows away. The barren desert expands into the space that once grew plants and supported farmers.

Over time, desertification can leave areas of the desert buried in sand.

The southern edge of the Sahara Desert is an area suffering from desertification. This part of the Sahara is growing at an amazing rate. In the last 50 years, the southern Sahara has sometimes increased by as much as 100 acres a day.

Wealth in the Desert

Great amounts of wealth can be found under the desert lands. The deserts of the American Southwest are known for gold and silver **deposits**. Diamonds are mined in South African deserts. One of the most important riches of the desert is oil. Much of the world's oil supply comes from deserts in the Middle East.

While gathering wealth from the desert may be necessary, it can cause problems in ecosystems. Plant and animal habitats are damaged or destroyed. Nomads are forced out of areas. Whole desert environments are changed when humans take over an area to remove precious **minerals**.

Dangers to Desert People

The San people of the Kalahari Desert are in danger of losing their lifestyle. Even though the San have lived in southern Africa for 20,000 years, the wealth of the desert is working against them.

The Kalahari Desert covers almost 70 percent of the country

of Botswana. It is suspected that diamonds and uranium are waiting to be discovered under the Kalahari. There is strong pressure to look for mineral wealth there.

Unfortunately, the Kalahari is home to the San people. They have used this land for centuries for their hunting and gathering. Their homes and communities may be in danger if the government takes over the land for mining. But the government of Botswana needs to think of all its people, not just the San.

The San people also compete with other tribes who lay claim to the desert. These tribes raise cattle for a living. As the edges of the Kalahari are overgrazed, the cattle-herding tribes demand more land from the San.

Nomads of the Future

In June and July of 1997, the Atacama Desert was explored in a new way. A team of scientists sent a robot named Nomad across the desert. As Nomad crossed the Atacama, scientists were able to gather information about the land, plants, and animals of the desert. A few years later, Nomad was sent to explore an area of the Antarctic Desert. In January of 2000, Nomad returned to Antarctica to look for meteorites, or rocks from outer space. Hopefully, future Nomad trips will continue to provide valuable information about the treasures of the desert biome.

The Nomad robot has studded tires for traction on the Antarctic ice and several cameras to record information in the desert.

Internet Connections and Related Reading for Deserts

http://mbgnet.mobot.org/sets/desert/index.htm

Take a trip through the desert. Learn about the deserts of the world and their plants and animals.

http://www.enchantedlearning.com/biomes/label/desert/

Use this printable map to label the major deserts using the clues provided.

http://www.enchantedlearning.com/biomes/desert/desert.shtml

This extensive site includes a map of the major deserts, a chart of the animals found in each desert, and in-depth information on many desert animals.

http://www.ucmp.berkeley.edu/glossary/gloss5/biome/deserts.html

Explore four types of deserts at this site.

http://desertusa.com/life.html

Discover the four North American deserts and the plants and animals that live there.

Cactus Hotel **by Brenda Z. Guiberson.** Brings to life a child's fantasies about the desert world and a giant saguaro cactus. Houghton Mifflin, 1993. [RL 2 IL K–3] (4534101 PB 4534102 CC)

The Desert Alphabet Book **by Jerry Pallotta.** The parched, mysterious deserts of the world are the landscapes for this alphabetic array of plants, animals, and phenomena. Charlesbridge Press, 1994. [RL 2 IL K–4]   (4691201 PB)

The Desert Is Theirs **by Byrd Baylor.** A lyrical description of the relationship between the desert and the many creatures, including humans, who live there. Macmillan, 1987. [RL 3 IL 1–4] (8675701 PB)

Deserts **by Neil Morris.** Looks at the various aspects of deserts, including natural features, wildlife, and the effects of humans. Includes index and glossary. Crabtree Publishing, 1996. [RL 4 IL 2–5] (4974301 PB 4974302 CC)

Deserts by Seymour Simon. Explains why and where deserts form, how the elements shape them, and how plants and animals adapt in order to survive. HarperCollins, 1997. [RL 5.4 IL K–5] (5543701 PB)

Desert Voices by Byrd Baylor. Desert inhabitants describe the beauty of their home. Macmillan, 1993. [RL 4 IL 1–5] (4463801 PB 4463802 CC)

Endangered Desert Animals by Dave Taylor. As desert areas are being developed into resorts, industrial cities, and oil towns, desert animals are losing the vegetation that once fed and sheltered them. Crabtree Publishing, 1993. [RL 4 IL 3–7] (4573601 PB 4573602 CC)

Mojave by Diane Siebert. From the tiny darting lizard to a galloping herd of wild mustangs, the sometimes unseen activity of the Mojave Desert is depicted in flowing verse. HarperCollins, 1992. [RL 3 IL K–4] (4333501 PB 4333502 CC)

One Day in the Desert by Jean Craighead George. Explains how the animal and human inhabitants of the Sonoran Desert of Arizona, including a mountain lion, a roadrunner, a coyote, a tortoise, and members of the Papago Indian tribe, adapt to and survive the desert's merciless heat. HarperCollins, 1996. [RL 3.1 IL 2–5] (4955701 PB 4955702 CC)

What Is a Biome? by Bobbie Kalman. This book introduces biomes, showing and describing the main kinds and discussing their location, climate, and plant and animal life. Crabtree Publishing, 1998. [RL 3 IL 2–5] (5729401 PB 5729402 CC)

Wonders of the Desert by Louis Sabin. A surprising number of creatures, including reptiles, insects, birds, and plants—each with its own special way of surviving the desert's harsh climate—live in this hot, dry land. Troll, 1982. [RL 3 IL 2–4] (8595001 PB)

•RL = Reading Level
•IL = Interest Level
Perfection Learning's catalog numbers are included for your ordering convenience.
PB indicates paperback. CC indicates Cover Craft. HB indicates hardback.

Glossary

adapt (uh DAPT) to learn to successfully live in an environment (see separate entry for *environment*)

adaptation (ad ap TAY shuhn) characteristic that helps an animal survive in its environment (see separate entry for *environment*)

Arctic Circle (ARK tik SER kuhl) area at the top of the globe that includes the North Pole, Arctic Ocean, and parts of Europe, Asia, and North America

barren (BAIR uhn) having little or no plants

barrier (BAIR ee er) object that blocks other objects

burrow (BER oh) hole in the ground where an animal lives

camouflage (KAM uh flahzh) protection due to coloring that blends in with the environment (see separate entry for *environment*)

coastal (KOH stuhl) near the coast, or shore, of a large body of water

community (kuh MYOU nuh tee) organisms that live together in a particular location (see separate entry for *organism*)

continent (KON ti nuhnt) one of the seven large areas of land on the Earth

coral reef (KOR uhl reef) rocky area in warm, shallow ocean waters created from the remains of animals called *polyps*

current (KER uhnt) movement or flow of water

deposit (dee PAHZ it) amount of a natural material, such as coal or oil, found in an area

environment (en VEYE er muhnt) set of conditions found in a certain area; surroundings

evaporate (ee VAP or ayt) to change from a liquid to a gas

hibernation (heye ber NAY shuhn) spending the winter in an inactive, or resting, state

mesa (MAY suh) small, flat-topped area of raised land

mineral (MIN er uhl) nonliving material found in nature

native (NAY tiv) originally living in an area

organism (OR guh niz uhm) living thing

plain (playn) flat, treeless land

plateau (plat OH) large raised area of land with a flat surface

precipitation (pree sip uh TAY shuhn) moisture that falls to the ground, such as rain or snow

rodent (ROH duhnt) small gnawing (biting or chewing with teeth) animal, such as a mouse, squirrel, or beaver

temperate (TEMP ruht) not extremely hot or cold

trench (trench) deep canyon on the ocean floor

trough (trawf) long, narrow pathway in the ground that can be deep or shallow

tundra (TUHN druh) treeless region with soil that is often frozen year-round

Index

acacias, 27
adaptations
    animal, 28–30
    human, 30–31
    plant, 26–28
adder snakes, 23
Arabian Desert, 11
arctic fox, 25
Atacama Desert, 17, 35
Australian deserts, 15, 17
biome (definition of), 5
    desert biome, 10
bobcats, 28–29
cactuses, 28
camels, 19–20
Chihuahuan Desert, 11, 16
climate, 14
coastal deserts, 17
cold deserts, 24–25
    Antarctica, 9, 11, 24–25, 35
    Greenland, 25
creosote bush, 27
darkling beetles, 22
Death Valley, 21
desert (definition of), 9
desert tarantulas, 29
desertification, 33–34
ecosystem (definition of), 6–7
    desert ecosystem, 10–11
fringe-toed lizards, 22–23
gerbils, 30
Great Basin, 16

hot and cold deserts, 22–23
    Gobi, 17, 23
    Namib, 17, 22–23
hot deserts, 18
    Mojave, 16, 21
    Sahara, 18–20, 34
    Thar, 20
jackrabbits, 29
Joshua Tree, 21
juniper trees, 27
kangaroo rats, 11
Kalahari Desert, 31, 34–35
lichens, 28
Mexican gold poppies, 11
minerals, 34
Mojave ground squirrels, 29
musk ox, 25
Nomad, 35
nomads, 30–31
    San culture, 31, 34–35
oases, 20
oleanders, 11
parakeets, 30
penguins, 24, 25
rain shadow deserts, 16–17
scorpions, 21
seals, 25
sidewinders, 21, 23
Sonoran Desert, 16
subtropical deserts, 15
Tropic of Cancer, 14, 15
Tropic of Capricorn, 14, 15
web-footed gecko, 23